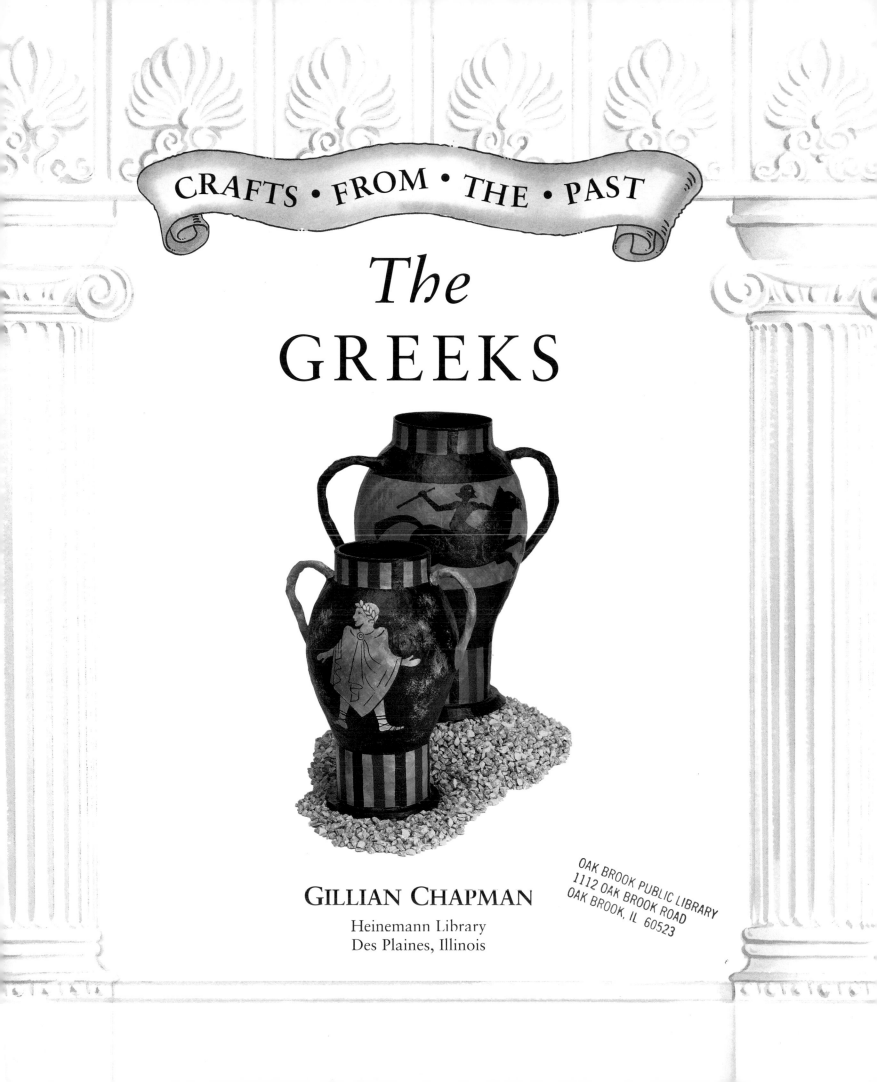

# CRAFTS · FROM · THE · PAST

# The GREEKS

## GILLIAN CHAPMAN

Heinemann Library
Des Plaines, Illinois

## GENERAL CRAFT TIPS AND SAFETY PRECAUTIONS

Read the instructions carefully, then gather everything you'll need
before you begin to work.

It will help if you plan your design first on scrap paper.

If you are working with papier-mâché or paint, cover the work surfaces
with newspaper.

Always use a cutting mat when cutting with a mat knife and ask
an adult to help if you are using sharp tools.

Keep paint and glue brushes separate and always wash them out after use.
Use non-toxic paints and glue.

Don't be impatient—make sure plaster is set, and papier-mâché or paint
is thoroughly dry before moving on to the next step!

All the projects make perfect presents!
Try to make them as carefully as you can.

## RECYCLING

Start collecting materials for craftwork. Save newspaper, colored
paper and cardboard, cardboard boxes and tubes of different sizes, magazines,
gift wrap, and scraps of string and ribbon.

Clean plastic containers and old utensils are perfect for mixing
plaster and making paper pulp.

## PICTURE CREDITS

**AKG Photos:** /Erich Lessing 6 bottom left, 36, /John Hios 6 bottom right: **British Museum:** 20, 22, 32, 34;
**C M Dixon:** 7 top left; **Michael Holford:** 7 bottom left, 8 top right, 8 bottom right, 8 bottom left, 10, 12, 14,
16, 18, 26; **Piraeus Museum, Athens:** 24; **Robert Harding:** 7 bottom right; **Science Photo Library:**
/John Sanford & David Parker 28; **Sonia Halliday Photographs:** /F. H. C. Birch 30.

©1998 Reed Educational & Professional Publishing
Published by Heinemann Library,
an imprint of Reed Educational & Professional Publishing,
1350 East Touhy Avenue, Suite 240 West
Des Plaines, IL 60018

Produced by Fernleigh Books
Designers: Gillian Chapman and Gail Rose
Photographer: Rupert Horrox
Illustrator: Teri Gower Picture Researcher: Jennie Karrach
© Fernleigh Books 1998
Printed in Hong Kong

03 02 01 00 99
10 9 8 7 6 5 4 3 2

The author and Fernleigh would like to thank the following:
Keith Chapman for all his help with the model making.

**Library of Congress Cataloging-in-Publication Data**
Chapman, Gillian.
  The Greeks / Gillian Chapman.
    p.   cm. — (Crafts from the past)
  Includes bibliographical references and index.
  Summary: Describes various aspects of life in ancient Greece and
provides instructions for creating related crafts, including
labyrinths, a bronze helmet, and a Trojan horse.
  ISBN 1-57572-733-1 (lib. bdg.)
  1. Handicraft—Greece—Juvenile literature.   2. Greece-
-Civilization—To 146 B.C.—Juvenile literature.  [1. Greece-
-Civilization—To 146 B.C. 2. Handicraft.]  I. Title.  II. Series.
TT75.C48    1998
938—dc21                 98-15668
                        CIP
                        AC

## Acknowledgments

Every effort has been made to contact copyright holders of any material
reproduced in this book. Any omissions will be rectified in subsequent printings
if notice is given to the publisher.

Some words are shown in bold, **like this**.
You can find out what they mean by looking in the glossary.

# CRAFTS · FROM · THE · PAST

# The GREEKS

## Gillian Chapman

# THE GREEK EMPIRE

THE LAND OF ANCIENT GREECE was a hot, mountainous **peninsula** surrounded by hundreds of small islands. Small isolated communities grew up all over this area, often cut off from each other by sea or mountains. These small communities grew into the Greek states which consisted of city-states supported by the surrounding countryside. Each independent state had its own laws and government.

Although the city-states, such as Athens and Sparta, were constantly quarreling among themselves, they were all united as Greeks. They all spoke the same language, worshiped the same gods and goddesses, and shared the same customs. They became a strong united force when they fought a common enemy, such as their victorious war against the Persians.

LEFT. *The city of Ephesus, in Asia Minor, had a huge sanctuary dedicated to Artemis, the Greek goddess of hunting.*

BELOW. ***Athens** was the most powerful city-state and the Athenians built temples to their gods and goddesses on the **Acropolis.***

6

# LAW, ORDER, AND KNOWLEDGE

ABOVE. **Aristotle** (384–322 B.C.) had a great love of knowledge. He was a politician, poet, scientist, and philosopher.

The idea of a **democratic** government was a Greek concept. The first democracy was established in Athens in 508 B.C. The Greeks enjoyed an ordered society in which individuals had great freedom and power. Creative thinking and personal achievements were encouraged. They admired the complete man—someone who was equally talented as an athlete, a poet, or a **philosopher**.

The Greeks excelled in many scientific areas, such as, astronomy, mathematics, and philosophy, which is the love of knowledge. They were a seafaring nation and needed the knowledge of astronomy for navigation. Greek architects relied on laws of **geometry** and mathematics for their engineering and building. Their styles of architecture influenced many cultures that followed after them.

LEFT. *The Treasury of the Athenians at Delphi.*

BELOW. *Fallen column drums at **Athens** show how the huge columns were constructed in sections.*

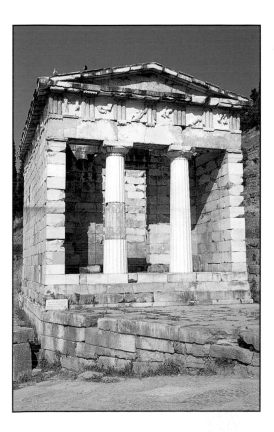

7

# ARTS AND CRAFTS

THE GREEK LOVE OF BEAUTY shows itself in their art and architecture. Sculpture was created in honor of the gods and goddesses and was displayed in temples and public buildings. It showed a perfect view of life—men with strong, healthy bodies, beautiful women draped in fine clothes, and strong horses carrying brave warriors. Skilled sculptors and artisans worked for patrons that demanded very high standards.

Poets were also held in high regard and the language of poetry, often set to music, developed into high forms of literature and theater which are still greatly admired today. Ancient legends and poems were memorized and passed on by storytellers. The most famous legends were written down by Homer in the *Iliad* and the *Odyssey*, and historians now believe that many of these epic tales are based on fact.

RIGHT. *A caryatid figure from the Erechtheum, the temple of Athena on the **Acropolis** at **Athens.***

BELOW LEFT. *The fourth century B.C. theater at Delphi.*

BELOW RIGHT. *Vase painting of the legends of Homer.*

# GREEK CRAFT TIPS

Painting and finishing projects is exciting. It is also the most difficult part, so take your time. By following these simple painting tips, everyone will be happy with the results.

Paint the masks in a dark color and leave to dry. Brush a lighter color on, leaving some of the dark paint showing through. Finally brush with gold paint to get a special effect.

Build up layers of different colored paint to achieve stunning effects. Keep the brush dry and use the paint sparingly. Don't draw in all the details if you don't want to!

Greek craftsmen were clever, but not at everything! Vases were made by a potter, but painted by an artist. When you paint pictures on a project, sketch the design first.

Don't be afraid to erase or start again. Only trace onto the project when the design looks right. Fix the tracing paper with tape to stop it from moving while you are tracing.

The Greeks believed that if something was worth doing, it was worth doing well. In the Greek spirit, try to make your projects as carefully as you can.

9

# DOLPHIN FRESCO

THE WALLS OF MANY TEMPLES and palaces were once decorated with beautiful **frescoes.** Originally these scenes were painted directly onto the wet plaster. However, over the centuries they have become damaged and many have been restored by modern artists re-creating fragments of the original frescoes.

There are many remains at the **Minoan** royal palace at Knossos, on the island of **Crete.** This fresco decorates the walls of the Queen's apartment.

The ancient Greek world was made up of the Greek mainland with its rugged coastline and many islands. Dolphins were often sighted in the warm coastal waters.

## DOLPHIN FRESCO

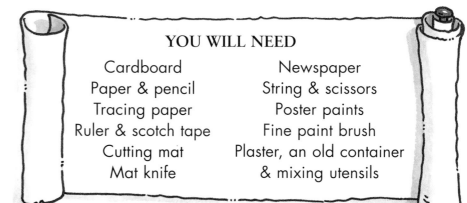

### YOU WILL NEED

| | |
|---|---|
| Cardboard | Newspaper |
| Paper & pencil | String & scissors |
| Tracing paper | Poster paints |
| Ruler & scotch tape | Fine paint brush |
| Cutting mat | Plaster, an old container |
| Mat knife | & mixing utensils |

1. Sketch your design on scrap paper using the ideas shown here. Copy the dolphins and the border patterns onto the fresco.

2. Measure the design and make a cardboard mold the same size, with sides 2 in. (5 cm) deep. Score the sides, turn them up, and tape together.

3. Mix the plaster in an old container, following the instructions on the package. Pour it into the mold to a depth of 1 1/4 in. (3 cm).

4. Smooth the surface of the plaster. Cut a 6 in. (15 cm) length of string and push the ends into the wet plaster, leaving a loop to hang the fresco up when it is dry.

5. When the plaster is dry, carefully remove it from the mold. Trace your dolphin design onto the smooth surface and pencil in the outlines.

6. Following the pencil outlines, carefully color in the dolphin design using poster paints and a fine brush. Try to follow the color scheme of the original fresco (far left).

11

# LABYRINTHS

THE ANCIENT GREEK LEGEND of the Minotaur tells of a monster—half man, half bull—who lived in a **labyrinth** on the island of **Crete.** Each year children were sacrificed to the monster until Theseus, the prince of **Athens,** decided to go to Crete to try and stop the killing.

The labyrinth was so complicated that no one had ever returned, but **Theseus** used a ball of string to mark his path. He bravely killed the Minotaur and used the string to retrace his steps.

The legend of Theseus killing the Minotaur was painted on this Greek vase in 450 B.C.

## ROLLING BALL PUZZLE

### YOU WILL NEED

| | |
|---|---|
| Shallow box with lid | Glue stick |
| Mat knife & cutting mat | Paints or felt tip pens |
| Cardboard | Paper scraps |
| Scissors | Colored marbles |
| Paper & pencil | String |

1. Design your puzzle so it is the same size as the bottom of the box. Incorporate into the design several places where the marbles must rest.

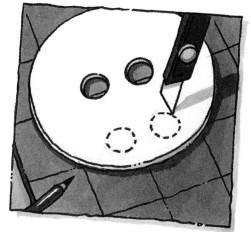

2. Cut out a piece of cardboard the same size as the design. Draw on the cardboard where the marbles will rest and cut the holes out neatly.

3. Carefully glue the cardboard into the bottom of the box and leave to dry. Then draw the puzzle design onto the cardboard with paints or felt tip pens.

4. Color the box and lid with poster paints or felt tip pens, or decorate it with the colored paper scraps.

5. Make a maze by gluing a coil of string into a box. Paint the string when the glue is dry and try guiding the marbles through the maze. How many can you get into the center of the spiral?

*Make it more difficult to roll marbles into the holes of the Minotaur puzzle by making the holes smaller and shallower.*

*When you are not playing with the maze or puzzle, replace the lid to keep the marbles safe!*

13

# TEMPLE COLUMNS

THE GREEKS BUILT magnificent temples to honor their gods and goddesses. Highly skilled craftsmen used only the finest materials. Some of the best examples of their work are the **Parthenon** and Temple of Athena (left) on the **Acropolis** in **Athens.**

Originally influenced by wooden buildings that had columns made from tree trunks, the Greeks discovered that stone columns could support much more weight. Columns were built from stacks of drum-shaped sections, held together with pegs. These were carved on site from marble or limestone and hauled into position by teams of workmen using ropes and pulleys.

The Greeks designed different styles of columns. Doric style columns have plain tops. Ionic columns are thinner with scrolled tops, like on the Temple of Athena.

## TEMPLE BOOKENDS

1. Plan the size of the bookend by positioning the four tubes on the empty tinfoil box, as shown above. If the box and tubes are too long, cut them down.

2. Fill the box with gravel or sand and seal up both ends using scotch tape. Use the box as a measure to cut out three pieces of thick cardboard exactly the same width and length.

3. Cut out four squares from one of the lengths of cardboard. Do the same with the second length. These squares will make the tops and bases for the columns.

*These temple bookends are an elegant and practical way to tidy up any book collection.*

*Paint the columns to look like real marble.*

4. Cover each of the cardboard tubes with corrugated paper. Cut the paper exactly to size. Then glue it to the tube, making sure it is firmly stuck down.

5. Assemble the bookend by gluing four squares of cardboard along the length of the box. Glue a column to each square. Make sure each column is secure.

6. Glue another square to the top of each column and finally attach the last card strip to the top. Cover all the flat surfaces with glued pieces of tissue. Then paint the bookend.

# THE OLYMPIC GAMES

THE OLYMPIC GAMES were held every four years at **Olympia,** in honor of **Zeus.** The first Games date back to 776 B.C., but sports competitions had been held among rival Greek cities for centuries.

The Greeks admired strength and physical fitness. As most boys were drafted into the army, sports like archery, boxing, fencing, and chariot racing all had a military use and trained the soldiers for war. Successful Olympic athletes were treated as heroes.

This picture painted on a vase in 510 B.C. shows an athlete holding weights that were used in long jumping.

## OLYMPIC PLATE

### YOU WILL NEED

| | |
|---|---|
| Compass | Paper plate |
| Thin cardboard | Orange, brown, |
| Scissors | & black paint |
| Glue stick | Paint brush |
| Pictures of | Paper & pencil |
| sports activities | Tracing paper |
| Black felt tip pen | |

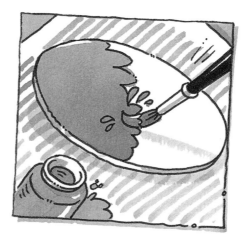

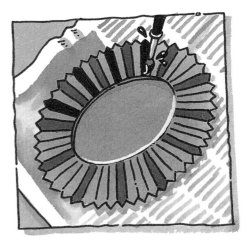

1. Use a compass to draw a circle on the cardboard. It will need to be the correct diameter to fit into the center of the paper plate.

2. Cut out the cardboard circle neatly with scissors. Then paint the circle using the orange paint. Cover the circle evenly with a thick coat.

3. Use the orange and brown paints to paint a border pattern on the paper plate. Let the paint dry, then finish the design with black paint.

4. Choose a sport and draw a design for the center of the plate on the paper. Either sketch a design or trace a picture from a magazine.

5. Make the design the same diameter as the cardboard circle. When you are happy with the design, trace it onto the orange cardboard circle.

6. Follow the lines of the traced design and draw over them with a black felt tip pen. Then glue the design to the center of the plate.

*Choose scenes from your favorite sports to decorate the plates.*

*There have been many changes in sports since the first Olympic Games!*

# PAINTED POTTERY

THE GREEKS WERE MASTER POTTERS and **Athens** was the center of pot production. Different vase painting styles evolved over the centuries with early vessels having geometric designs.

Then around 720 B.C. a style known as the "black figure technique" developed, where figures were painted black against a red clay background. Later, in 500 B.C., the process was reversed and "red figure" vases became the fashion. Many beautiful vases have survived over thousands of years.

Try making some Greek pots from papier-mâché. Paint the black-figure and red-figure techniques on different shaped vases.

## PAINTED VASE

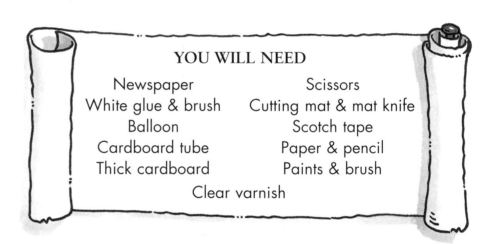

**YOU WILL NEED**

| | |
|---|---|
| Newspaper | Scissors |
| White glue & brush | Cutting mat & mat knife |
| Balloon | Scotch tape |
| Cardboard tube | Paper & pencil |
| Thick cardboard | Paints & brush |
| Clear varnish | |

1. Blow up the balloon. Tear the newspaper into small paper strips. Dilute the white glue and use it to cover the balloon with six layers of paper strips.

2. When the paper strips are dry, pop the balloon and remove it. Make the vase shape by taping a section of cardboard tube to the top and bottom, and a circle of thick cardboard to the base.

3. Neaten all the joints by pasting strips of paper across and cover the complete vase with a layer of pasted strips. Roll up a length of newspaper to make the handles.

We can learn much about the Greeks from the details painted on their pottery, such as, the style of their clothing, their armor, and weapons.

4. Cut the handles to size and glue them in place, making sure they are secure. Cover them with strips of glued paper, especially where they join the vase.

5. When all the glue is dry, paint the vase white. Now it is ready for painting. Sketch your design on scrap paper before painting the vase.

Either use the ideas shown here or look in books about the Greeks. You will find many beautiful examples of painted vases and different shapes to make.

A coat of clear varnish will help to protect your vases.

*Vases were painted with pictures of heroes, athletes, and actors, as well as scenes from everyday life.*

# TERRA-COTTA TOYS

THE ANCIENT GREEKS were well-known for their sophisticated painted vases and plates (see page 18) that were beautifully shaped and decorated. But they also made much simpler forms of pottery. Some date back to the eighth century B.C., when the Greek nation started to expand and trade with other **Mediterranean** countries.

**Terra-cotta** pots were made to contain oils, perfumes, and wine. Simple clay figures and animals were made as toys for children to play with. A clay doll with moving limbs was found with its own small chair and tiny boots.

Terra-cotta toys, like this horse and rider, were found buried in children's graves.

## TERRA-COTTA HORSE

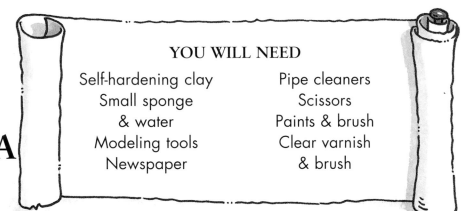

### YOU WILL NEED

Self-hardening clay
Small sponge & water
Modeling tools
Newspaper

Pipe cleaners
Scissors
Paints & brush
Clear varnish & brush

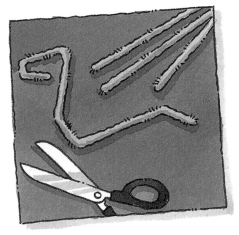

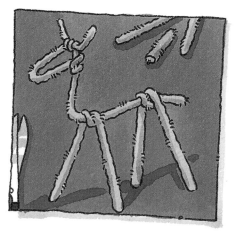

1. Look at the shapes of the clay animals opposite. Cut the pipe cleaners to the right length to make a framework for your model.

2. Bend a pipe cleaner to make the body and head shape. Twist lengths of pipe cleaner around the body to make the legs and ears.

3. Cover the work surface with newspaper. Knead some clay in your hands to make it soft. Then start to cover the pipe cleaners with small pieces.

*Try making several terra-cotta horses and riders.*

*Make the riders in the same way, building up the clay over pipe cleaner shapes.*

4. Build up the horse shape, pressing the clay into the pipe cleaners to make it stick. Keep the clay damp with the wet sponge as you work.

5. When you have modeled the horse into the right shape, smooth the surface all over using your fingers and the wet sponge.

6. Leave the horse in a safe place to dry. Then paint it with simple patterns. Give it two coats of clear varnish to help protect it.

# GOLDEN TREASURE

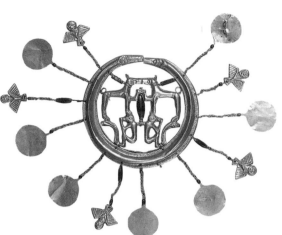

Look carefully at the earring above and see the dogs, owls, monkeys, and snake that shape the design.

THE GREEKS ADMIRED BEAUTIFUL SCULPTURE, works of art—and beautiful people. But physical beauty was for the wealthy. Men kept their bodies healthy and strong through sports. Rich women wore fine clothes, perfume, and gold jewelry.

This golden earring is part of a collection of jewelry called the Aigina Treasure. The treasure was named after the Greek island where it was found. The treasure includes bracelets, brooches, and belts. It was made by skilled goldsmiths in about 1700 B.C. from beaten gold, gold wire, and precious stones.

# GOLDEN CHARM BRACELET

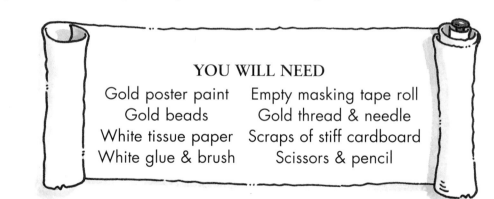

## YOU WILL NEED

| | |
|---|---|
| Gold poster paint | Empty masking tape roll |
| Gold beads | Gold thread & needle |
| White tissue paper | Scraps of stiff cardboard |
| White glue & brush | Scissors & pencil |

1. Brush white glue over an area of the empty masking tape roll, then stick small pieces of white tissue paper to it.

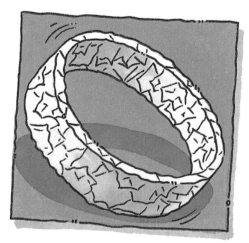

2. Completely cover both sides of the roll with several layers of the glued tissue pieces and leave to dry.

3. Cut out a number of shapes from the cardboard—circles, stars, diamonds, and moons. Make a hole in each with the needle.

4. Paint the bracelet with gold poster paint and then paint all the cardboard shapes on both sides.

5. Sew a length of gold thread through each charm. Attach gold beads to the thread and tie each thread to the bracelet.

6. Make some more charms and tie them to a pair of gold earrings so they match the charm bracelet.

*Try making a charm bracelet for someone special.*

*Make the charms to suit different people by using animal or flower shapes.*

# GREEK THEATER

GREEK THEATERS were huge outdoor auditoriums. The design of the theater meant that thousands could see the performance.

Actors also wore thick-soled boots and padded costumes to appear larger. Male actors played all the roles and clay masks were worn to identify characters. Some masks had two faces so an actor could quickly change moods. Other masks had funnel shaped mouths that projected the voices.

Expressions were greatly exaggerated on the masks so that they could be seen from a distance.

## TRAGIC AND COMIC MASKS

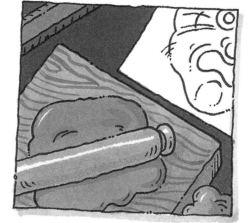

1. First you will need to sketch the mask design on paper. Decide whether your mask will be tragic or comic. Make a life-size sketch and draw in all the features.

2. Roll out the modeling clay on the board using the rolling pin. Following your design, model the clay until it takes on the shape and size of your mask design.

3. When the mask is the right size, add more pieces of clay and shape the features. Don't forget that all traditional Greek masks had very exaggerated features.

*Make small holes in
each side of the mask and thread
through the thin elastic so you can
wear it or hang it on the wall.*

*Look at the
painting techniques
explained on page 9.*

4. Tear up a quantity of small strips of newspaper. Use a diluted solution of white glue and cover the mold with six layers of paper. Make sure each layer covers evenly.

5. Leave the mask to dry completely, then remove it from the mold. Trim around the mask with scissors and cut out the eyes and mouth holes with a mat knife.

6. Now the mask is ready for painting. Use your imagination to paint it in the colors you think express the emotion—whether it's a comic mask or a tragic mask!

# BRONZE HELMET

YOUNG GREEK SOLDIERS joined the army at age eighteen, but they had to provide their own armor and weapons. Soldiers from wealthy families that could afford strong metal body armor became **"hoplites."** The well-armed hoplites were a powerful fighting force.

The helmet was the hoplite's most important piece of armor. Most Greek designs completely covered the head. They had nose and cheek protectors and small openings for the eyes and mouth. Some bronze helmets had large plumes of colored horse hair.

This bronze helmet was made in 460 B.C. and comes from **Olympia,** where it would have been given to the god **Zeus** as an offering.

# GREEK HELMET

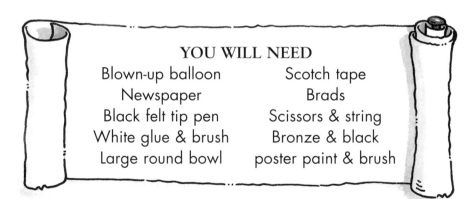

**YOU WILL NEED**

| | |
|---|---|
| Blown-up balloon | Scotch tape |
| Newspaper | Brads |
| Black felt tip pen | Scissors & string |
| White glue & brush | Bronze & black |
| Large round bowl | poster paint & brush |

1. To make the helmet shape, glue torn newspaper pieces all over the blown-up balloon with white glue. Cover with three layers of newspaper.

2. Then cover only the top of the balloon with three more layers of newspaper pieces. Leave the balloon in a safe place to dry and then pop it.

3. Draw the outlines of the eye holes and nose piece on the surface. Cut this shape out using scissors and cut around the base of the helmet.

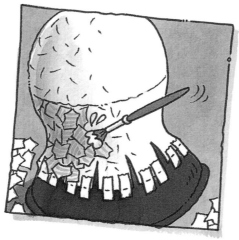

4. Cut some slits in the sides of the helmet and carefully splay it open—remember the helmet is very thin here! Push the helmet over a large round bowl to keep this curved shape.

5. Tape the helmet to the bowl to keep it firmly in place. Continue gluing three more layers of newspaper pieces to the bottom part of the helmet covering the slits. Leave to dry.

6. Neaten the bottom of the helmet. Decorate with lengths of glued string and brads. Cover the ends of the brads inside the helmet with strips of glued paper.

*Do not worry if your helmet has some dents—these "battle scars" will make it look even more realistic!*

*Paint the helmet with bronze and black poster paints.*

# STARS OF THE ZODIAC

THE ANCIENT GREEKS had a great love of wisdom. They believed that science and the observation of the stars would give them a greater understanding of the whole universe. Some famous Greek scientists were Pythagoras, Archimedes, and **Hippocrates.**

There are twelve constellations in the Zodiac. They circle the Earth each year and your star sign is the one that coincides with your birthday. Above is the constellation of Leo, the lion.

Over 2,000 years ago Greek astronomers identified many star constellations and named them after their **mythological** creatures and heroes. **Ptolemy** listed forty constellations including Orion and the Great Bear.

## ZODIAC CARDS

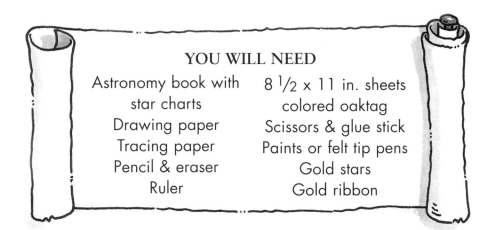

### YOU WILL NEED
Astronomy book with star charts
Drawing paper
Tracing paper
Pencil & eraser
Ruler

8 1/2 x 11 in. sheets colored oaktag
Scissors & glue stick
Paints or felt tip pens
Gold stars
Gold ribbon

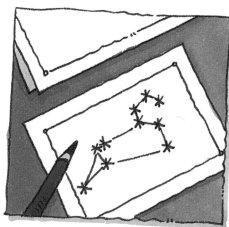

1. Fold one of the sheets of oaktag in half to make your card. Draw a 1/2 in. (15 mm) border on the front of the card. This is the space for the zodiac design.

2. Look through the astronomy book and choose one of the zodiac constellations to draw. Make a sketch of the stars, but make sure your drawing is the correct size to fit on the card.

3. The zodiac constellations are named after a particular creature. Draw the outline of the animal around the stars. Refer to your book as certain stars represent a leg or a tail.

Make one of these unusual Zodiac cards for a friend's birthday.

"Zodiac" comes from the Greek word meaning animal.

4. Take time when you draw. Don't be afraid to erase parts and redraw them. When you are happy with it, use the tracing paper to trace it onto the front of the card.

5. You can either color in your design using the felt tip pens or paints. Alternatively, cut out the main animal shape from colored oaktag and decorate it with smaller cut-out shapes.

6. Stick gold stars to the card in the places where the real stars are in the constellation. Finally, decorate the border design and glue a gold ribbon onto the front.

# TROJAN HORSE

THE LEGEND OF THE TROJAN HORSE tells the story of the Greek army that had besieged the city of **Troy** for ten long years. They were ready to accept defeat, but their leader **Odysseus** had a clever idea.

Trojan soldiers saw that the Greek army had set sail leaving behind a huge wooden horse. The Trojans dragged it into the city thinking it was a prize and that the Greek army were defeated. That night soldiers hidden in the horse opened the gates for the Greek army who had quietly returned and they destroyed the city.

## TROJAN GIFT HORSE

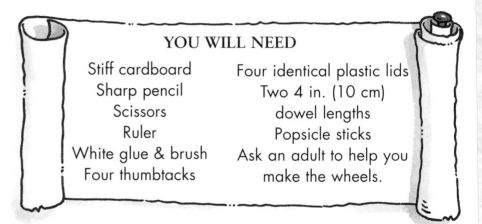

### YOU WILL NEED

Stiff cardboard
Sharp pencil
Scissors
Ruler
White glue & brush
Four thumbtacks

Four identical plastic lids
Two 4 in. (10 cm) dowel lengths
Popsicle sticks
Ask an adult to help you make the wheels.

1. Fold the cardboard in half and draw the simple shape on one side. Cut out the shape, cutting through both thicknesses of cardboard. Be very careful not to cut along the fold.

2. Cut two slits in the top fold of cardboard. Then mark the wheel holes on the folded shape. Pierce through both sides of card with a sharp pencil. Make sure the holes line up.

3. Cut out a piece of cardboard 3 in. (8 cm) wide but narrower than the horse. Score and fold it as shown and glue it inside the body of the horse to form the secret compartment.

4. Cut small lengths of popsicle stick to size. Glue them to the lids and leave to dry in a safe place. You may need an adult to help you carefully push a thumbtack through the center of each lid.

5. Decorate the horse's body with glued pieces of popsicle stick. Attach a lid to a piece of dowel with a thumbtack. Thread the dowel through the holes, then tack a lid to the other end. Repeat for the second axle.

6. Draw the horse's head on a folded piece of cardboard. Cut out the shape, being careful not to cut along the fold. Decorate the head with pieces of popsicle stick and glue it to the body.

*Priam, the Trojan king, ignored the warning, "Fear the Greeks bearing gifts." But why not make a Trojan gift horse and hide a nice surprise inside?*

*Add small pieces of popsicle stick to make a mane and tail, and paint the horse.*

31

# MEDUSA AND PERSEUS

**MEDUSA** was a terrible monster in Greek **mythology**. She had poisonous snakes in her hair and a gaze that turned living things to stone. Perseus was sent to bring her head back.

The Greek gods hated Medusa and decided to help Perseus by giving him special gifts—a polished shield, a **sickle**, a pair of winged sandals, and a helmet that made him invisible. Perseus was able to get close to Medusa without looking at her by using the shield as a mirror. He cut off her head with the sickle.

Medusa's sisters tried to catch Perseus, but he used his magic helmet and winged sandals and flew away unseen.

## MEDUSA MIRROR

### YOU WILL NEED

| | |
|---|---|
| Newspaper | Circular mirror |
| Two large bowls | (without a frame) |
| (or containers) | Stiff cardboard & ruler |
| Hot water | Compass |
| White glue & brush | Mat knife & cutting mat |
| Paints & brush | String & scissors |
| Rubber gloves | |

1. Make the paper pulp by tearing up small pieces of newspaper into a bowl. Cover the paper pieces with hot water and leave them to soak overnight.

2. Wearing rubber gloves, take handfuls of wet paper, squeeze out the water and put it in the second bowl. Use your hands to mash it together with white glue, until it feels soft and smooth.

3. Measure the width of your circular mirror and add 4 in. (10 cm) to the measurement. Then draw a circle of this size onto a sheet of stiff cardboard using the compass.

*Make sure all the snakes are dry before painting them in ghastly colors!*

*Make a hole at the top of the mirror—and hang it in the bathroom. Then everyone can look like Medusa first thing in the morning!*

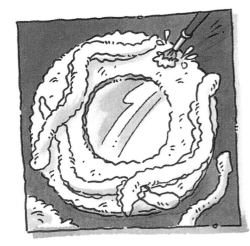

4. Take time to carefully cut out the cardboard circle using the mat knife and cutting mat. Glue the mirror to the center of the cardboard with glue and leave it in a safe place to dry.

5. Take small lumps of pulp and press them onto the cardboard, building up a textured frame around the mirror. Brush on extra glue to help the pulp stick to the cardboard.

6. Model lumps of pulp into snake shapes and glue them around the mirror. You may need to let some snakes dry before trying to glue others over the top of them!

33

# THE MINOANS

**CRETE** is the largest of the Greek islands. It was one of the great centers of culture during the fifteenth century B.C. The **Minoan's** lived on Crete—they were named after the island's king, Minos.

The bull was considered a sacred animal and was worshiped by the Minoans. During festivals, offerings were made to the bulls and acrobats, and dancers performed dangerous feats, leaping over the horns of galloping bulls and dancing on their backs.

This clay bull's head was used to sprinkle water as part of a religious ritual during festivals.

# MINOTAUR HEAD

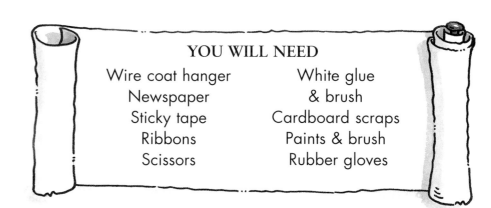

**YOU WILL NEED**

| | |
|---|---|
| Wire coat hanger | White glue |
| Newspaper | & brush |
| Sticky tape | Cardboard scraps |
| Ribbons | Paints & brush |
| Scissors | Rubber gloves |

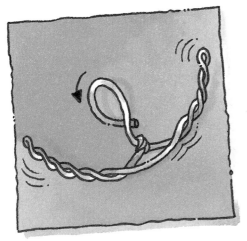

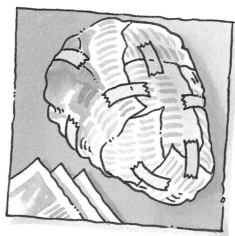

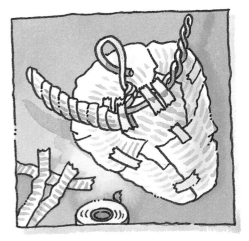

1. You will need some help to bend the coat hanger. Twist the sides together, bend them into a curved shape around the hook and bend the hook into a loop.

2. Scrunch several sheets of newspaper together to make a head shape. Add more sheets until the head is the right size and tape them firmly together.

3. Tape the hanger to the back of the head, then cover the wire with strips of paper taped into place. These are the bull's horns, so add paper until they are thick enough.

 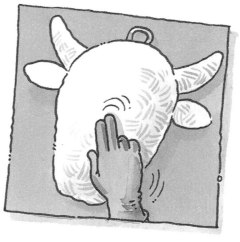 

4. Tape two cardboard ear shapes to the head and cover the head with several layers of torn paper, glued with white glue.

5. Smooth over the final layer of paper with your fingers and leave the bull's head in a safe place for the glue to dry.

6. Paint the whole head pale brown and then decorate it with painted patterns. Use the wire loop to hang the head.

*You could hang lightweight objects over the horns or decorate the head with colorful ribbons.*

# CYCLADIC STATUES

THE GREEKS sculpted magnificent bronze and marble statues in honor of their gods, goddesses, and heroes. Sculptors followed strict rules of **proportion** and carved goddess and athletes with beautiful faces and perfect bodies.

But 2,000 years before the age of classical beauty and **realism**, sculptors of the Cycladic Islands in the Aegean Sea carved very simple marble statues to honor their gods. Many figures have been excavated from burial sites or found by divers on the sea floor. All are very similar in their shape, style, and simplicity.

## CYCLADIC FIGURE

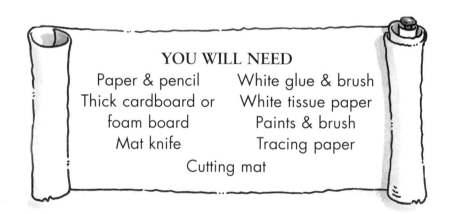

**YOU WILL NEED**

| | |
|---|---|
| Paper & pencil | White glue & brush |
| Thick cardboard or foam board | White tissue paper |
| | Paints & brush |
| Mat knife | Tracing paper |
| Cutting mat | |

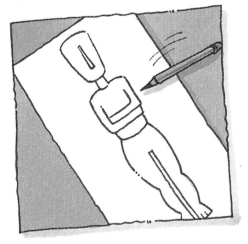

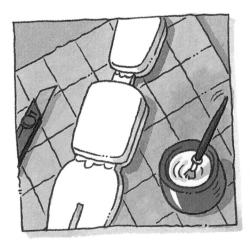

1. Make a sketch of the figure on paper. Look at the examples shown here. Keep the figure very simple. Draw in the nose and arms.

2. Carefully trace the outline of the figure onto the thick cardboard or foam board. Foam board is ideal to use as it is easier to cut out.

3. Now cut out the figure. Make the body and head thicker by cutting out another layer of board and glue these in place with white glue.

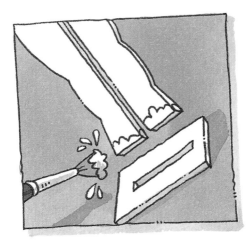

4. Cut out shapes for the nose and arms and glue these to the figure. Cut out a square of board for a base. Make a slot in the base for the feet to fit into and glue them in place.

5. Cover the whole figure with small pieces of white tissue, glued with white glue. The tissue will soften the shape and give the figure an interesting texture.

When the glue is dry, paint the figure to look like marble.

*Genuine Cycladic figures are priceless, but these models look very convincing!*

*Cycladic statues are tall, but very thin when looked at from the side.*

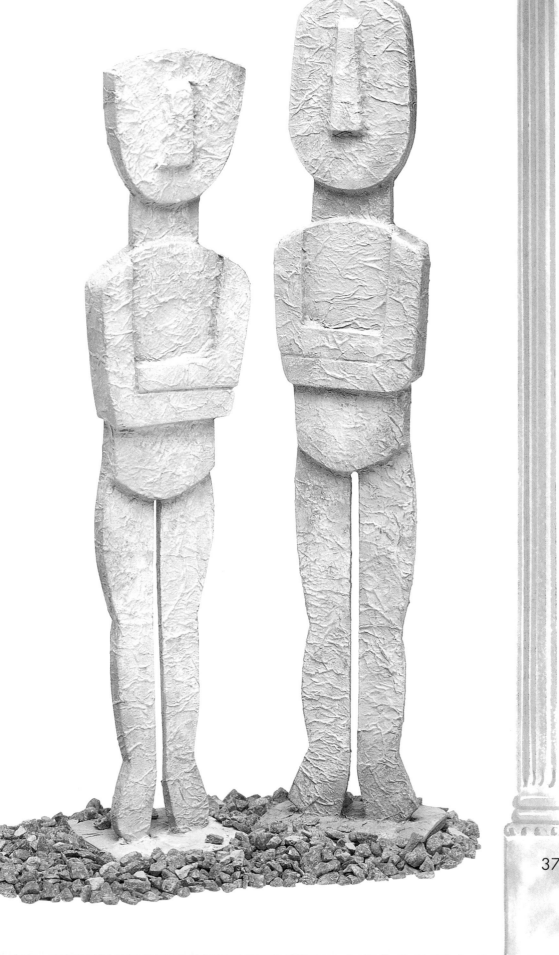

# GLOSSARY

**Acropolis** – a defensive fort or citadel usually built on the highest point of a city. The hilltop acropolis in **Athens** is also where the Athenians built their temples to the gods

**Aristotle** – a Greek politician and philosopher who lived between 384 and 322 B.C.

**Athens** – the most important and wealthiest city-state in ancient Greece, famed as a center for art and culture

**Crete** – the largest island in the Aegean Sea that formed part of Ancient Greece

**Democracy** – a state or country that is ruled by the people where they vote for a leader. This type of government was first utilized in the Greek city-states

**Fresco** – a large painting decorating walls or ceilings made by applying paint directly onto wet plaster

**Geometry** – math that deals with measurements and relationships of lines, angles, and solids

**Hippocrates** – a Greek doctor who lived between 460 and 377 B.C. He believed in treating the whole body and is known as the founder of modern medicine

**Hoplites** – well-armed foot soldiers of the Greek army

**Labyrinth** – a large maze. The labyrinth on **Crete** was the home of the Minotaur and was impossible to escape from

**Mediterranean** – the name given to the sea and the lands and countries surrounding it

**Medusa** – a **mythological** creature. One of the Gorgons, it was half woman—half serpent, whose hair was full of writhing snakes and whose gaze turned men to stone

**Minoan** – the ancient civilization on **Crete.** It was named after its king, Minos, and reached its peak between 2200 and 1450 B.C.

**Mythological** – fictional stories about gods and heroes that have been retold through time

**Odysseus** – a Greek hero, whose adventures, including the capture of **Troy,** were written down by Homer

**Olympia** – the Greek city that held the athletic games in honor of **Zeus** every four years

**Parthenon** – large temple built on top of the **Acropolis** for the goddess Athena

**Peninsula** – an area of land that is surrounded by water on three sides

**Philosophy** – the study resulting from the love of knowledge and wisdom

**Proportion** – Greek sculptors devised ways of measuring the body so every part looked perfect and was in proportion to the whole

**Ptolemy** – a Greek astronomer. Around A.D. 100 he used mathematics to explain the movement of the planets

**Realism** – a style of art where sculpture and painting is made to look as realistic as possible

**Sickle** – a sharp curved tool used by to cut straw and wheat

**Terra-cotta** – word meaning "burned earth." Terra-cotta is a form of red clay used for making pottery

**Theseus** – the young prince of **Athens,** who killed the Minotaur in the **Labyrinth**

**Troy** – an ancient city on the west coast of modern Turkey. The Greeks and Trojans were at war for ten years

**Zeus** – the chief of all the Greek gods. The Greeks believed he was the sender of thunder, lightning, and winds